CHEROKEE PSALMS

A Collection Of Hymns in the Cherokee Language

Translated by
Daniel Scott

Designed & Edited by
J. Ed Sharpe

CHEROKEE PUBLICATIONS
CHEROKEE N.C.
1991

ONE DROP OF BLOOD

ga do da juh ya
duh ne li ji sa
o ga je li ja guh wi yoo hi
o ga li ga li
yuh ha gwo ye no
jo gi luh wi sda ne di yi.

o ga je li ga
ja guh wi yoo hi
ja je li ga no
ja guh wi yoo hi,
o ga je li ga
ja guh wi yoo hi
ja je e li ga
ja guh wi yoo hi.

ᎦᏙᏓ ᏨᏯ
ᏛᏁᎵ ᏥᏌ
ᎣᎦᏤᎵ ᏣᎬᏫᏳᎯ
ᎣᎦᎵᎦᎵ
ᏴᎭᏉᏰᏃ
ᏦᎩᎸᏫᏍᏓᏁᏗᏱ.

ᎣᎦᏤᎵᎦ
ᏣᎬᏫᏳᎯ
ᏣᏤᎵᎦᏃ
ᏣᎬᏫᏳᎯ,
ᎣᎦᏤᎵᎦ
ᏣᎬᏫᏳᎯ
ᏣᏤᎡᎵᎦ
ᏣᎬᏫᏳᎯ

(Tune not available)

It is told, by the old Cherokees in Oklahoma, that this is the song that was sung by the Cherokee people during their forced removal, which is known to the Cherokees as the "TRAIL OF TEARS". It was in the years l838-l839 when the United States Government, under Andrew Jackson, uprooted the Cherokees from their traditional home in the East and marched them to a strange land by way of Tennessee, Kentucky, Illinois, Missouri, Arkansas, and then into the Indian Territory (now Oklahoma).

The Cherokees were allowed only the clothes on their backs and the march commenced about November 3, l838 and terminated at Fort Gibson, Indian Territory in March/April l839. More than 5,000 Cherokees died on the way.

TABLE OF CONTENTS

Note: * MBST = May Be Sung To The Tune Of Songs Noted

ᏣᎳᎩ ᏗᏕᎶᏆᏍᏗ

CHEROKEE SYLLABARY

Ꭰ a		Ꭱ e	Ꭲ i	Ꭳ o	Ꭴ oo	Ꭵ uh
Ꭶ ga	Ꭷ ka	Ꭸ ge	Ꭹ gi	Ꭺ go	Ꭻ goo	Ꭼ guh
Ꭽ ha		Ꭾ he	Ꭿ hi	Ꮀ ho	Ꮁ hoo	Ꮂ huh
Ꮃ la		Ꮄ le	Ꮅ li	Ꮆ lo	Ꮇ loo	Ꮈ luh
Ꮉ ma		Ꮊ me	Ꮋ mi	Ꮌ mo	Ꮍ moo	
Ꮎ na		Ꮑ ne	Ꮒ ni	Ꮓ no	Ꮔ noo	Ꮕ nuh
Ꮏ hna	Ꮐ nah					
Ꮖ qwa		Ꮗ qwe	Ꮘ qwi	Ꮙ qwo	Ꮚ qwoo	Ꮛ qwuh
Ꮜ sa	Ꮝ s	Ꮞ se	Ꮟ si	Ꮠ so	Ꮡ soo	Ꮢ suh
Ꮣ da		Ꮥ de	Ꮧ di	Ꮩ do	Ꮪ doo	Ꮫ duh
Ꮤ ta		Ꮦ te	Ꮨ ti			
Ꮬ dla	Ꮭ tla	Ꮮ tle	Ꮯ tli	Ꮰ tlo	Ꮱ tloo	Ꮲ tluh
Ꮳ ja	Ꮴ je	Ꮵ ji	Ꮶ jo	Ꮷ joo		Ꮸ juh
Ꮹ wa		Ꮺ we	Ꮻ wi	Ꮼ wo	Ꮽ woo	Ꮾ wuh
Ꮿ ya		Ᏸ ye	Ᏹ yi	Ᏺ yo	Ᏻ yoo	Ᏼ yuh

KEY TO PRONUNCIATION

a = a(rt) ga = ga(r) ka = ka(rt) la = la(rk) ......through...... ya = ya(rn)

e = e(rr) ge = ge(cko) ke = ke(lly) le = le(t) ....through...... ye = ye(ll)

i = i(t) gi = gi(ddy) ki = ki(t) li = li(t) ....through...... yi = yi(ppee)

o = o(pen) go = go(at) ko = ko(la) lo = lo(de).......through...... yo = yo(lk)

oo = oo(ps) goo = goo(p) koo = koo(l) loo = loo(m)...through...... yoo = yoo(p)

uh = uh-huh.....nasalised. All syllables ending in uh

NOTE: The Cherokee are the only Native American people to have a written syllabary. Its eighty-five symbols represent every sound in the Cherokee language. It was written by George Gist, better known by his Cherokee name of Sequoyah . He is the only man in history to have invented a written language in its entirety even though he, himself, could not read or write in any language. This syllabary was completed in 1821 after twenty years of labor. He often met with severe resistance from members of his own family and his own tribe who did not understand what he was doing. Sequoyah died alone in Mexico while searching for members of his tribe thought to have migrated there. The site of his grave is unknown.

PSALM 139

May be sung to:

I Shall Be At Home With Jesus
Come, Thou Fount
Brethren, We Have Met To Worship
I Will Arise And Go To Jesus

1. yi ho wa ja ne hla nuh hi,
ha dluh wuh da ji lo si
da guh ya di sga la ne li ?
ja na ye hi sdi ni hi.

i yoo ye no go luh la di
yi na gwa duh ne ta nuh,
na hna yi sgi go wa ti ha
na hna ye no di jo hla.

2. joo ni yo hoo suh di ne huh
na sgwo yi wa gi lo suh ,
a si gwo yi sgi go wa ti,
ni ga ni duh i he hi.

a me gwo hi no wa sduh i
i yoo yi wa gwa duh nuh
na hna yi sgwa ti ni do ha,
a le yi do sgi ni yuh.

3. i yoo a le duh gwoo tluh ni
li si gi ya gwa duh nuh
na sgwo oo li si gi ge suh
i ga hi yoo gwo yi gi.

tle sdi guh sga nuh je luh gi;
tla ye no hi luh hi tluh
yuh ga guh ya di sga la si,
ja na ye hi sdi ni hi.

Translation:

PSALM 139

O Lord, Thou hast searched me, and known me. Thou knowest my downsitting and mine uprising: Thou understandest my thoughts afar off. Thou compassest my path and my lying down, and art acquainted with all my ways. For there is not a word in my tongue, but, lo, O Lord, Thou knowest it altogether. Thou hast beset me behind and before, and laid thine hand upon me. Such knowledge is too wonderful for me; it is high, I cannot attain unto it. Whither shall I go from thy spirit? or whither shall I flee from thy presence? If I ascend up into heaven, Thou art there: if I make my bed in hell, behold, Thou art there. If I take the wings of the morning, and dwell in the uttermost parts of the sea; even there shall Thy hand lead me, and Thy right hand shall hold me.

If I say, surely the darkness shall cover me; even the night shall be a light about me. Yea, the darkness hideth not from Thee: but the night shineth as the day: the darkness and the light are both alike to thee.

For Thou hast possessed my reins: Thou hast covered me in my mother's womb. I will praise thee; for I am fearfully and wonderfully made: marvelous are Thy works: and that my soul knoweth right well. My substance was not hid from Thee, when I was made in secret, and curiously wrought in the lowest parts of the earth. Thine eyes did see my substance, yet being unperfect; and in Thy book all my members were written, which in continuance were fashioned, when as yet there was none of them.

How precious also are Thy thoughts unto me, O God! how great is the sum of them! If I should count them, they are more in number than the sand; when I awake, I am still with Thee. Surely Thou wilt slay the wicked, O God: depart from me, therefore, ye bloody men.

For they speak against Thee wickedly, and Thine enemies take Thy name in vain. Do I not hate them, O Lord, that hate Thee? and am not I grieved with those that rise up against Thee? I hate them with perfect hatred; I count them mine enemies. Search me, O God, and know my heart: try me, and know my thoughts: And see if there be any wicked way in me, and lead me in the way everlasting.

THE BROAD AND THE NARROW WAY

May be sung to the tune: **Higher Ground**

1. nuh no hi a hya te ni yoo
juh sgi no wi ga nuh hnuh i;
oo ni ja ta no na ne hi
yuh wi oo na de do wa di.

ji sa sgi ni i ga se he
a ya to li ga nuh hnuh i,
a ne do ha sgi ni na hna
i di tluh a ni ga yo hli.

2. sgi sda wa doo ga a di ha
ho wa i ja doo li sge sdi
ga luh la di to hi jo suh
i juh ya li sgo da ne luh.

de ji yo sge sdi e lo hi
a le ni ga di yoo oo dli
i ji ye luh hi, a di ha
ka ne guh i gi sde li sgi.

3. ki lo joo ya we i sdi yoo
yoo ye luh oo ne hla nuh hi
oo je li a sda wa di suh
a le yi a soo li go ga.

oo dio na sdi sgi ni na sgi
oo da nuh ti oo je luh hi,
oo yo i yoo li sda ne di
tla oo dia si duh hi yi gi.

4. sgwa ne hla nuh hi uh tle sdi
ya gwa dio na sta ne sdi gwo;
a le oo too gi a gwuh suh
tle sdi a se yi ge se sdi.

a ni soo li go gi sgi ni
a le wo oo na dlo na sdi
noo no sduh i tle sdi a yuh
na sgi gwo yi na gwa sde sdi.

Translation:

Enter ye in at the straight gate: for wide is the gate, and broad is the way that leadeth to destruction, and many there be which go in thereat: because strait is the gate, and narrow is the way, which leadeth unto life, and few there be that find i t.

The Lord said, "Follow me, (I am the way, the truth, and the life). Forsake the world and all that is in it. (So likewise, whosoever he be of you that forsaketh not all that he hath he cannot be my disciple)."

But he, who has given up the world and and worldly things and doubts not, is of the Lord`s. (But the scripture hath concluded all under sin, that the promise by faith of Jesus Christ might be given to them that believe).

He is my Lord and I am a debtor to Him (for I was under the wrath of Almighty God until the only begotten of the Father gave His life on the cross and paid my debt).

GUIDE ME, JEHOVAH

1. sgwa ti hni se sdi yi ho wa
e la di ga i suh i
ji wa na ga hli yoo a yuh
ja hli ni gi di ni hi.

ni go hi luh, ni go hi luh,
sgi sde li sge sdi yo go
ni go hi luh, ni go hi luh,
sgi sde li sge sdi yo go.

2. nuh wo ti ga noo go guh i
a nuh wo sgi sdoo i si
a ji luh no oo lo gi luh
i guh yi a i se sdi.

sgi sde li sgi, sgi sde li sgi,
di sgi ga na wa di da
sgi sde li sgi, sgi sde li sgi,
di sgi ga na wa di da.

3. ga la si nuh oo wa tla uh
jo da ni oo we yuh i
sgi yo hi sda ne luh gwo no
a gwe li hi sdi sguh i

sgi sde li sgi, sgi sde li sgi,
to hi de sgi sa sda nuh
ni go hi luh, ni go hi luh,
to da guh no gi sta ni.

COME, THOU FOUNT

Tune only

1. Come, thou fount of every blessing,
Tune my heart to sing Thy grace;
Streams of mercy, never ceasing,
Call for songs of loudest praise.

Teach me some melodious sonnet,
Sung by flaming tongues above;
Praise the mount I'm fixed upon it.
Mount of Thy redeeming love.

2. Here I raise mine Ebenezer;
Hither by Thy help I'm come;
And I hope, by Thy good pleasure,
Safely to arrive at home.

Jesus sought me when a stranger,
Wandering from the fold of God;
He, to rescue me from danger,
Interposed His precious blood.

3. O to grace how great a debtor
Daily I'm constrained to be!
Let Thy goodness, like a fetter,
Bind my wandering heart to Thee:

Prone to wander, Lord, I feel it,
Prone to leave the God I love;
Here' s my heart, O take and seal it:
Seal it for Thy courts above.

May also be sung to: **Tell It Everywhere You Go.**
What A Friend We Have In Jesus.
Precious Memories.
Any common meter song 8-6 / 8-6

Translation:

Take us and guide us, Jehovah, as we are walking through this barren land. We are weak, but Thou art mighty. Ever help us.

Open unto us Thy healing waters (Living Waters). Let the fiery cloud (Thy Holy Spirit) go before us, and continue Thy help.

Help us when we come to the verge of the Jordan River (death), and we shall for eternity sing Thy praise.

PSALM 139

1 yi ho wa ja ne hla nuh hi
ha dluh wuh da ji lo si
da guh ya di sga la ne li ?
ja na ye hi sdi ni hi.

i yoo ye no ga luh la di
yi na gwa duh ne ta nuh,
na hna yi sgi go wa ti ha
na hna ye no di jo hla.

2. joo ni yo hoo suh di ne huh
na sgwo yi wa gi lo suh,
a si gwo yi sgi go wa ti,
ni ga na duh i he hi.

a me gwo hi no wa duh i
i yoo yi wa gwa duh nuh
na hna yi sgwa ti ni do ha,
a le yi do sgi ni yu h.

3. i yoo a le duh gwoo tluh ni
li si gi ya gwa duh nuh
na sgwo oo li si gi ge suh
i ga hi yoo gwo yi gi.

tle sdi guh sga nuh je luh gi;
tla ye no hi luh hi tluh
yuh ga guh ya di sga la si,
ja na ye hi sdi ni hi.

COME, THOU FOUNT

Tune only

1. Come, Thou fount of every blessing,
Tune my heart to sing Thy grace;
Streams of mercy, never ceasing,
Call for songs of loudest praise.

Teach me some melodious sonnet,
Sung by flaming tongues above;
Praise the mount -- I' m fixed upon it
Mount of Thy redeeming love.

2. Here I raise my Ebenezer;
Hither by Thy help I'm come;
And I hope, by Thy good pleasure,
Safely to arrive at home.

Jesus sought me when a stranger,
Wandering from the fold of God;
He, to rescue me from danger,
Interposed His precious blood.

3. O to grace how great a debtor
Daily I'm constrained to be !
Let Thy goodness, like a fetter,
Bind my wandering heart to Thee:

Prone to wander, Lord, I feel it,
Prone to leave the God I love;
Here's my heart, O take and seal it;
Seal it for Thy courts above.

Translation: Psalm l39. See page 5.

HEAVENLY HOME

May be sung to the tune **A Beautiful Life**

1. oo wo doo ha (oo wo doo ha) di gwe nuh suh (di gwe nuh suh),
a gi li ya (a gi li ya) noo we huh na (noo we huh na),
nuh do a ji (nuh do a ji) go na duh di (go na duh di)
noo ne gi yuh (noo ne gi yuh) a da ne luh (a da ne luh).

Chorus:
(di gwe nuh suh) di gwe nuh suh (wi ji ga ti) wi ji ga ti,
(ta li ne yuh) ta li ne yuh (ga ji yo hoo) ga ji yo hoo ,
hna gwo a se (hna gwo a se) wi ji ga ti (wi ji ga ti),
ta li ne yuh (ta li ne yuh) ga ji yo oo (ga ji yo oo)

2. no gwi si doo (no gwi si doo) go na duh di (go na duh di),
e do do yi (e do do yi) di gwe nuh suh (di gwe nuh suh),
ga luh la di (ga luh la di) yoo ge suh i (yoo ge suh i);
na hna tle gi (na hna tle gi) wi ji loo ji (wi ji loo ji)

3. wa na ne sguh (wa na ne sguh) li e lo hi (li e lo hi),
a go huh sgi (a go huh sgi), a yo gi no (a yo gi no),
a yuh sgi ni (a yuh sgi ni) ga soo ya gi (ga soo ya gi),
ga luh lo juh (ga luh lo juh) di da ne luh (di da ne luh).

4. wa li na hi (wa li na hi) sda e lo hi (sda e lo hi),
nuh do no wa (nuh do no wa) ni sgo luh gi (ni sgo luh gi),
a le ni ga (a le ni ga) di go tluh nuh (di go tluh nuh),
di gwe nuh suh (di gwe nuh suh) yuh guh yo gi (yuh guh yo gi).

Translation:

My heavenly home is a beautiful place, it is brighter than the sun. I am going there when I leave this world (die). It shall be much better to be in my heavenly home, and I shall be there soon.

We can begin to build our heavenly home while we are still on this earth (by the life we live in the service of our Lord and Saviour Jesus Christ) by the deeds we do in His Holy Name. It is a mansion not built with hands and it outshines the sun.

NOTE: phrases in ( ) for bass voice and in some tunes for alto

MEETING OF CHRISTIANS

1. di ga da ge yoo hi,
   no hi de da dlo hi;
   ga luh la di oo wa suh hi
   di ge nuh suh jo suh.

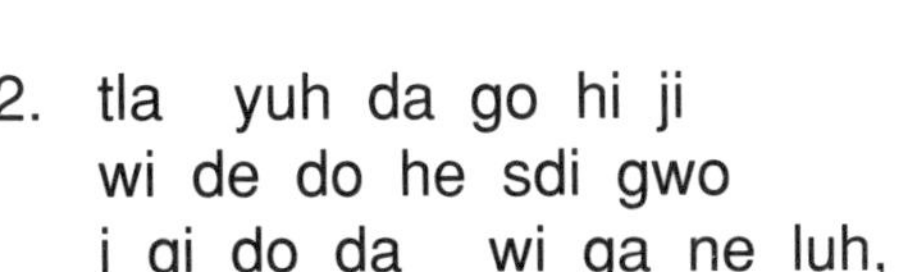

2. tla yuh da go hi ji
   wi de do he sdi gwo
   i gi do da wi ga ne luh,
   ga luh la di jo suh.

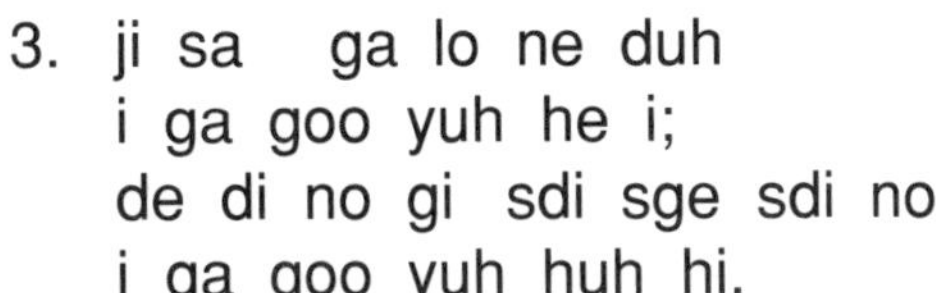

3. ji sa ga lo ne duh
   i ga goo yuh he i;
   de di no gi sdi sge sdi no
   i ga goo yuh huh hi.

4. ga luh la di he hi,
   sgi sde li sge sdi gwo;
   di jo hluh i wo ji ga ti
   ga luh la di jo suh.

BLEST BE THE TIE THAT BINDS

I. Blest be the tie that binds,
   Our hearts in Christian love;
   The fellowship of kindred minds
   Is like to that above.

2. Before our Father's throne
   We pour our ardent prayers;
   Our fears, our hopes, our aims are one,
   Our comforts, and our cares.

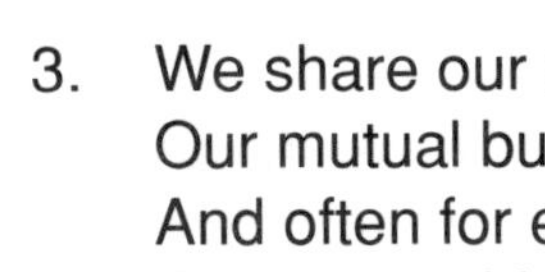

3. We share our mutual woes,
   Our mutual burdens bear;
   And often for each other flows
   The sympathizing tear.

4. When we asunder part,
   It gives us inward pain;
   But we shall still be joined in heart,
   And hope to meet again.

Translation:

We, that love one another, have come together in this meeting. The fellowship of kindred minds is like to that in heaven.

It will not be long when we shall be at our Father's throne in heaven.

Jesus Christ our Lord paid the price for our reconcilliation to God our Father. Let us sing His praises for His finished work on the cross at Calvary for our justification.

It will only be a short time when we shall meet in heaven where we shall live in peace for eternity.

Thou, who art in heaven, we pray thatThou wilt continue to help us. We are going, by the grace of God, to where Thou art sitting on Thy throne in heaven.

ALAS! AND DID MY SAVIOUR BLEED

l. a gi sde li sgi ji hi i
gi guh oo je wo je (le),
ji sga nuh a goo yi sge i
oo li sgwa de le i.

chorus:
oo ja ti oo wo doo na ni we (a)
na hna ni, i ga do joo luh sa duh
jo suh i, ge na ni wi ga ga noo go
guh i, joo wo doo hi do di da ne luh.

2. ji sga na hi yoo ge suh i
ge duh a ga duh ne (i),
noo yo tle noo li sda ne le (i).
a gi sde li sge sdi.

3. ka luh i oo sgo luh je i
hna gwo oo li sgwa de (luh)
yuh wi oo ni sga nuh juh hi
de a goo yuh sge i.

4. hna gwo ga da nuh te sguh i
ga duh ji go wa duh,
di ji sga do li oo ja do
a ma de e go i.

5. ge uh i de guh ya hi si
sgi yo hoo hi se luh (hi),
na sgi gwo oo wa suh hi yoo
i guh gwa duh ne di.

AT THE CROSS

1. Alas, and did my Saviour bleed?
And did my sovereign die?
Would He devote that sacred head
For such a worm as I?

chorus:
At the cross, at the cross where I first
saw the light, and the burden of my heart
rolled away, it was there by fai th I
received my sight, and now am happy all
the day !

2. Was it for crimes that I have done,
He groaned upon the tree?
Amazing pity! Grace unknown!
And love beyond degree!

3. Well might the sun in darkness hide,
And shut his glories in,
When Christ, the Mighty Maker, died
For man the creature's sin.

4. But drops of grief can ne'er repay
The debt of love I owe:
Here, Lord, I give myself away,
'Tis all that I can do!

(It takes five Cherokee verses to translate four English verses.)

The Cherokee is direct translation of
AT THE CROSS

JESUS MY ALL

1. oo ne hla nuh hi oo we ji
jo suh i na gwo woo lo suh,
ji ya li sga sdo di na sgi,
woo lo suh wuh da ji lo si.

a ya to li wi ga nuh hnuh,
oon da nuh ti woo ni lo suh (i),
oo ne hla nuh hi joo wo hluh
na gwo a se wi ji ga ti.

2. oo dli hi gwo ji sga nuh go
ga dli ni guh ne ho (no) a se,
hna gwo no ji ya duh sga nuh
oo ne hla nuh hi oo we ji.

e he na oo duh hnuh ji sa;
o si yoo a gi ye luh nuh,
joo wo hluh wa gi lo suh gi,
de a gwa da ni luh yuh gi.

3. hna gwo do da ji na ne li
a ni sga na a ne huh i,
oo ne hla nuh hi oo we ji
ji no hi ji ji wa tuh huh.

oo ne hla nuh hi oo we ji
je ja ga nuh ga i ka li (i),
oo ja ti oo gi li yo je
ni hi i ja goo yi sge i.

SWEET HOUR OF PRAYER

Tune only

1. Sweet hour of prayer! Sweet hour of prayer!
That calls me from a world of care,
And bids me at my Father's throne
Make all my wants and wishes known;

In seasons of distress and grief,
My soul has often found relief,
And oft escaped the tempter's snare
By thy return, sweet hour of prayer.

2. Sweet hour of prayer! Sweet hour of prayer!
Thy wings shall my petition bear
To Him whose truth and faithfulness
Engage the waiting soul to bless;.

And since He bids me seek His face,
Believe His word and trust His grace,
I'll cast on Him my every care,
And wait for thee, sweet hour of prayer.

3. Sweet hour of prayer**!** Sweet hour of prayer!
May I thy consolation share,
Till, from Mount Pisgah's lofty height,
I view my home, and take my flight:

This robe of flesh I'll drop, and rise
To seize the everlasting prize;
And shout, while passing through the air,
Farewell, farewell, sweet hour of prayer.

Translation:

The Son of God (Jesus Christ our Lord) has returned to heaven. I shall go to be with Him when my life is over in this world. The way is narrow to the throne of God; the meek who have departed, have gone that way, and are now at our Father's throne. I, also, am going that way.

According to my nature, I was by choice an enemy of God and was afar off. But Jesus said, "come" (by the grace of God and through mercy) I believed and delighted in His call to come to Him. I shall go to be with Him.

And I will tell of the Son of God to those who are still living in unrighteousness. I shall tell them of my Saviour and what He has done for me.

The Son of God laid down His life that the scriptures should be fulfilled, He paid the price (for redemption) in full.

GUIDE ME, JEHOVAH

May be sung to the tune **Tell It Everywhere You Go**

1 sgwa ti hni se sdi, yi ho wa
e la di ga i suh i;
ji wa na ga hli yoo a yuh,
ja hli ni gi di ni hi

ni go hi luh
** (ni go hi luh, ni go hi luh)

sgi sde li sge sdi yo go,

ni go hi luh
** (ni go hi luh, ni go hi luh)

sgi sde li sge sdi yo go.

1. ᏍᏆᏘᏂᏎᏍᏗ, ᏱᎰᏩ,
ᎡᎳᏗ ᎦᎢᏒᎢ;
ᏥᏩᎾᎦᏝᏳ ᎠᏴ,
ᏣᏝᏂᎩᏗ ᏂᎯ.

ᏂᎪ ᎯᎷ
ᏂᎪᎯᎷ, ᏂᎪᎯᎷ

ᏍᎩᏍᏕᎵᏍᎨᏍᏗᏲᎪ,

ᏂᎪ ᎯᎷ
ᏂᎪᎯᎷ, ᏂᎪᎯᎷ

ᏍᎩᏍᏕᎵᏍᎨᏍᏗᏲᎪ.

2. nuh wo ti ga luh go guh i
a nuh wo sgi sdoo i si;
a ji luh no oo lo gi luh
i guh yi a i se sdi

sgi sde li sgi
** (sgi sde li sgi, sgi sde li sgi)

di sgi ga na wa di da,

sgi sde li sgi
** (sgi sde li sgi, sgi sde li sgi)

di sgi ga na wa di da.

2. ᏄᏬᏘ ᎦᎷᎪᎬᎢ
ᎠᏄᏬ ᏍᎩᏍᏙᎢᏏ;
ᎠᏥᎷᏃ ᎤᎶᎩᎷ
ᎢᎬᏱ ᎠᎢᏎᏍᏗ.

ᏍᎩᏍᏕ ᎵᏍᎩ
ᏍᎩᏍᏕᎵᏍᎩ, ᏍᎩᏍᏕᎵᏍᎩ

ᏗᏍᎩᎦᎾᏩᏗᏓ,

ᏍᎩᏍᏕ ᎵᏍᎩ
ᏍᎩᏍᏕᎵᏍᎩ, ᏍᎩᏍᏕᎵᏍᎩ

ᏗᏍᎩᎦᎾᏩᏗᏓ.

3. ga la si nuh oo wa tla guh
jo da ni oo we yuh i
sgi yo hi sda ne luh gwo no
a gwe li hi sdi sguh i;

** sgi sde li sgi
** (sgi sde li sgi, sgi sde li sgi)

to hi de sgi sa sta nuh
ni go hi luh
** (ni go hi lih, ni go hi luh)

to da guh no gi sta ni.

*** Bass & alto only.*

3. ᎦᎳᏏᏄ ᎤᏩᏢᎬ
ᏦᏓᏂ ᎤᏪᏴᎢ,
ᏍᎩᏲᎯᏍᏓᏁᎷᏉᏃ
ᎠᏇᎵᎯᏍᏗ ᏍᎬᎢ;

ᏍᎩᏍᏕ ᎵᏍᎩ
ᏍᎩᏍᏕᎵᏍᎩ, ᏍᎩᏍᏕᎵᏍᎩ

ᏙᎯ ᏕᏍᎩᏌᏍᏔᏅ

ᏂᎪ ᎯᎷ
ᏂᎪᎯᎷ, ᏂᎪᎯᎷ

ᏙᏓᎬᏃᎩᏍᏔᏂ.

See also page 24

Translation :

Take me and guide me, Jehovah, as I am walking through this barren land. I am weak, but Thou art mighty. Ever help me.

Open unto us Thy healing waters (Living Waters). Let the fiery cloud (Thy Holy Spirit) go before us and continue Thy help.

Help us when we come to the verge of the Jordan River (death), and we shall for eternity sing Thy praise.

PSALM 139

1. yi ho wa ja ne hla nuh hi
   ha dluh wuh da ji lo si
   da guh ya di sga la ne li ?
   ja na ye hi sdi ni hi.

chorus
   i yoo ye no ga luh la di
   yi na gwa duh ne ta nuh,
   na hna yi sgi go wa ti ha
   na hna ye no di jo hla.

2. joo ni yo hoo suh di ne huh
   na sgwo yi wa gi lo suh,
   a si gwo yi sgi go wa ti,
   ni ga na duh hi he hi.

chorus:
   a me gwo hi no wa sduh i
   i yoo yi gwa duh nuh,
   na hna yi sgwa ti ni do ha,
   a le yi do sgi ni yuh.

3. i yoo a le duh gwoo tluh ni
   li si gi ya gwa duh nuh,
   na sgwo oo li si gi ge suh
   i ga hi yoo gwo yi gi.

chorus:
   tle sdi guh sga nuh je luh gi
   tla ye no hi luh hi tluh
   yuh ga guh ya di sga la si,
   ja ni ye hi sdi ni hi.

Translation: Psalm 139. See page 5.

ᏚᏕᏏ ᎾᏧᏚᏚᏂ ᏤᎾᏥ ᏆᏉᎴᏝᏍᏕ
ᎠᏆᏂᎪᎯᏍᏗᏍᎩ ᎤᏁᎳᏅᎯ
ᎠᎩᏍᏕᎸᏍᎩ. ᎾᏍᎩ ᏚᏬᏢᏁ
ᎦᎸᎳᏗ ᎠᎴ ᎡᎶᎯ

ᏚᎾ ᏗᎧᏃᎩᏛ

I WILL ARISE AND GO TO JESUS

Tune only

1. Come, ye sinners, poor and needy,
   Weak and wounded, sick and sore;
   Jesus ready stands to save you,
   Full of pity, love and power.

chorus:
   I will arise and go to Jesus,
   He will embrace me in His arms,
   In the arms of my dear Saviour,
   Oh, there are ten thousand charms.

2. Come, ye thirsty, come, and welcome,
   God's free bounty glorify;
   True belief and true repentance,
   Every Grace that brings you nigh.

3. Come, ye weary, heavy laden,
   Lost and ruined by the fall;
   If you tarry till you're better,
   You will never come at all.

4. Let not conscience make you linger,
   Nor of fitness fondly dream;
   All the fitness He requireth,
   Is to feel your need of Him.

Also may be sung to the tune:
Brethren We Have Met To Worship

I WILL LIFT UP MINE EYES UNTO THE HILLS, FROM WHENCE COMETH MY HELP. MY HELP COMETH FROM THE LORD, WHICH MADE HEAVEN AND EARTH.

PSALM 121:1-2

CHRIST'S SECOND COMING

May be sung to the tunes: **Amazing Grace** *fast chorus*
It Came Upon The Midnight Clear
How I Love Jesus (There Is A Name I Love To Hear)

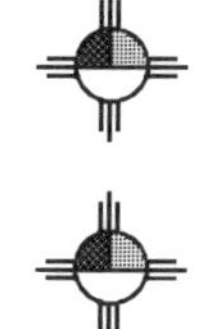

1. oo ne hla nuh hi oo we ji
   i ga goo yuh he i,
   hna gwo jo suh wi oo lo se
   i ga goo yuh ho nuh.

ᎤᏁᎳᏅᎯ ᎤᏪᏥ
ᎢᎦᎫᏴᎮᎢ,
ᏁᏆ ᏦᏒ ᏫᎤᎶᏎ
ᎢᎦᎫᏴᎰᏅ.

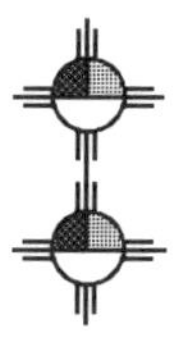

chorus
a se no i oo ne je i
i yoo no doo le nuh,
ta li ne duh ji loo ji li,
oo duh hne oo hne juh.

ᎠᏎᏃ ᎢᎤᏁᏤᎢ
ᎢᏳᏃ ᏚᎴᏅ,
ᏔᎵᏁ ᏛᏥᎷᏥᎵ,
ᎤᏛᏁ ᎤᏁᏨ.

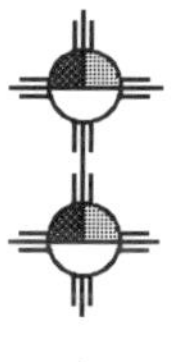

oo na da nuh ti a ne huh
do duh ya nuh hi li,
jo suh na gwo ni go hi luh
to hi wa ne he sdi.

ᎤᎾᏓᏅᏘ ᎠᏁᎲ
ᏙᏛᏯᏅᎯᎵ,
ᏦᏒ ᎾᏉ ᏂᎪᎯᎸ
ᏙᎯ ᏩᏁᎮᏍᏗ.

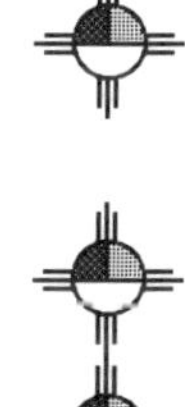

2. e la ni guh duh li sgwa di
   ga loo juh ha i yoo;
   ni ga duh da ye di go i
   a hni e la ni guh.

ᎡᎳᏂᎬ ᏛᎵᏍᏆᏗ
ᎦᎷᏨᎭ ᎢᏳ;
ᏂᎦᏛ ᏓᏰᏗᎪᎢ
ᎠᏂ ᎡᎳᏂᎬ.

Translation:

The Son of God paid the price for our redemption. When He finished (His death, burial and ressurection), making the payment, and He ascended into heaven(after forty days).

But before He ascended into heaven, He said, "Let not your heart be troubled; ye believe in God, believe also in me. In my Father's house are many mansions: if it were not so, I would have told you. I go to prepare a place for you. And if I go to prepare a place for you, I will come again, and receive you unto myself, that where I am, there ye may be also."

And when he comes again, (Beloved, now we are the sons of God, and it doth not yet appear what we shall be, but we know that, when he shall appear, we shall be like Him) we shall see Him as He is.

And all they who live in righteousness of the Lord Jesus Christ, and shall continue in love, will live in peace in heaven for eternity.

PSALM 146

1. a gwa ne hla nuh hi
ji luh gwo di
ni go hi luh e lo -
hi ge uh i,
guh wo la de sguh no
a li sgwa duh
a si no de ji no -
gi sdi sge sdi.

2. tla i luh hi yoo yuh -
guh li sgwa di
oo ne hla nuh hi ji -
luh gwo di sguh,
tla ni go hi luh e -
la di ge uh,
a le tla guh ni duh
di ge suh i.

3. o si i yoo li sda -
ne di ki lo
yi ho wa ja li sga -
sdo di sgo i;
ni guh na duh ye no
oo ne hla nuh,
a le ni guh na di -
i a ne huh.

4. oo ne hla nuh wi na -
sduh na e ha,
wi na sduh na oo hli -
ni gi di yoo;
na sgi ga luh gwo di
oo ne juh i
uh tla a se gwo yi -
nuh ga li sta.

BREAK THOU THE BREAD OF LIFE

Tune only

I. Break Thou the bread of life,
Dear Lord, to me,
As Thou didst break the loaves
Beside the sea;
Beyond the sacred page
I seek Thee, Lord;
My spirit pants for Thee,
O living Word.

2. Bless Thou the truth, dear Lord
To me, to me,
As Thou didst bless the bread
By Galilee;
Then shall all bondage cease,
All fetters fall;
And I shall find my peace,
My all in all.

3 Thou art the bread of life,
O Lord to me,
Thy holy word the truth
That saveth me;
Give me to eat and live
With Thee above;
Teach me to love Thy truth,
For Thou art love.

4. O send Thy spirit, Lord,
Now unto me,
That He may touch my eyes,
And make me see:
Show me the truth concealed
Within Thy Word,
And in Thy Book revealed
I see the Lord.

Translation: **PSALM 146**

Praise ye the Lord. Praise the Lord, O my soul. While I live will I praise the Lord: I will sing praises unto God while I have my being.

Put not your trust in princes, nor in the son of man, in whom there is no help. His breath goeth forth, he returneth to his earth; in that very day his thoughts perish.

Happy is he that hath the God of Jacob for his help, whose hope is in the Lord his God: whichmade heaven and earth; the sea, and all that therein is: which keepeth truth for ever: which executeth judgement for the oppressed: which giveth food to the hungry.

The Lord looseth the prisoners; the Lord openeth the eyes of the blind: the Lord raiseth them that are stooped down: the Lord loveth the righteous: the Lord preser√´th the strangers; he reli´√´†h the fatherless and widow: but the way of the wicked he turneth upside down.

The Lord shall reign for ever, even thy God, O Zion, unto all generations. Praise ye the Lord.

PSALM 103

1. oo sgwa da nuh do hna gwo
hi luh gwo da
oo da do li ja ti oo ne hla nuh hi
a le tle sdi juh ke wi suh
ni ga duh
o si a ye luh di ja do li juh i.

2. ni ga duh ja sga nuh juh ja do li gi,
a le na sgwo ja tluh guh
ja nuh wi sgi,
a le ni ga duh ja li sde luh do di
ni go hi luh ja li sgo luh da ne hi.

3. ga ni li yoo oo ta la wo hi sdi yi

oo ga do li ja duh oo ka li juh hi;
ga luh lo (i) e lo (hi) ji noo go na
duh di
na sgi yi ho wa noo da do li ja ta.

4. Nuh do di ga noo go guh nuh do no i

woo de li guh ji ni doo da luh na sgi
i yuh duh yi ho wa i gi huh e luh

oo ja ti oo yo i gi sga nuh juh i.

.

5. a ga yuh li ge joo na sdi joo we ji
oo ja ta nuh (hi) ji de ga do li ga i,
na sgi ya oo guh wi yoo hi yi ho wa,

ni de ga do li go guh wa na ye sgi.

HOW FIRM A FOUNDATION

Tune only

I. How firm a Foundation, ye saints of the Lord,

Is laid for your faith in His excellent Word!
What more can He say than to you He hath said,
You who unto Jesus for refuge have fled?

2 In poverty's vale, or abounding in wealth;
At home and abroad, on the land, on the sea,
As your days may demand, shall your strength ever be.

3. "When through fiery trials thy pathway shall lie,
My Grace, all sufficient, shall be thy supply;
The flames shall not hurt thee; I only design

Thy dross to consume and thy gold to refine."

4. " E'en down to old age, all my people shall prove
My sovereign, eternal, unchangeable love;
And when hoary hairs shall their temples adorn,
Like lambs they shall still in my bosom be borne."

5. "The soul that on Jesus had leaned for repose,
I will not, I will not desert to its foes;
That soul, tho all hell should endeavor to shake,
I'll never, no, never, no, never forsake."

Translation: PSALM 103

Bless the Lord, O my soul: and all that is within me, bless His Holy Name. Bless the Lord, O my soul, and forget not all His benefits: Who forgiveth all thine iniquities; who healeth all thy diseases; who redeemeth thy life from destruction; who crowneth thee with lovingkindness and tender mercies; who satisfieth they mouth with good things; so that thy youth is renewed like the eagle's.

The Lord executeth righteousness and judgement for all that are opressed. He made known His ways unto Moses, His acts unto the children of Israel.

The Lord is merciful and gracious, slow to anger, and plenteous in mercy. He will not always chide: neither will He keep His anger forever. He hath not dealt with us after our sins; nor rewarded us according to our iniquities. For as the heaven is high above the earth, so great is His mercy toward them that fear Him.

COME, WE THAT LOVE THE LORD

l. ka e di ge yoo i
ga luh la di he hi,
i da li e li je he sdi
i da li e li je he sdi
de di no gi sdi sguh,
de di no gi sdi sguh.

chorus
sa ya ni i de ga
oo wo doo hi yoo sa yan
sa ya ni no i de ga
yi ho wa oo je li.

2. i ga ne hla nuh hi,
wi na sduh na je ha,
hna gwo a se i gi do da,
hna gwo a se i gi do da,
a le i gi li i
a le i gi li i.

3. joo ne je li da sdi
do da ka ne je li,
do da ge ga ti ne si no,
do da ge ga ti ne si no.
wo wo hluh jo suh i,
wo wo hluh jo suh i.

4. yi ho wa oo je li
ga da de ga la sga
joo we nuh suh ga luh la di,
joo we nuh suh ga luh la di;
wi ga na noo go gi,
wi ga na noo go gi.

WE'RE MARCHING TO ZION

Tune & translation

1. Come, we that love the Lord,
And let our joys be known,
Join in a song with sweet accord,
Join in a song with sweet accord.
And thus surround the throne,
And thus surround the throne.

chorus
We're marching to Zion,
Beautiful, beautiful Zion;
We're marching upward to Zion,
The beautiful city of God.

2. Let those refuse to sing
Who never knew our God;
But children of the heavenly King,
But children of the heavewnly King,
May speak their joys abroad,
May speak their joys abroad.

3. The hill of Zion yields
A thousand sacred sweets
Before we reach the heavenly fields,
Before we reach the heavenly fields,
Or walk the golden streets,
Or walk the golden streets.

4. Then let our songs abound,
And every tear be dry;
We're marching thro' Immanuel's ground,
We're marching thro' Immanuel's ground,
To fairer worlds on high,
To fairer worlds on high.

JUST AS I AM

1. na gwa sduh gwo ga ji sga ni,
   ja gi guh a gwa li sga sdo duh,
   a le sgi ya ni sguh ji sa,
   wi ji loo ji, wi ji loo ji.

2. na gwa sduh gwo sgi sde li sgi,
   ni ji ga ti di sguh na no,
   ji sga nuh a gi huh sdi yi,
   wi ji loo ji, wi ji loo ji.

3. na gwa sduh gwo a gi hyo i,
   guh ni duh a gwa doo li sguh,
   a le ni ga uh gwo, ji sa,
   wi ji loo ji, wi ji loo ji.

4. na gwa sduh gwo a se ni hi,
   da sgi do li ji gwo a yuh,
   a le sgi sde luh di ji sa,
   wi ji loo ji, wi ji loo ji.

JUST AS I AM

Tune and translation

I. Just as I am, without one plea,
   But that Thy blood was shed for me,
   And that Thou bidd'st me come to Thee,
   O Lamb of God, I come! I come!

2. Just as I am, and waiting not,
   To rid my soul of one dark blot,
   To Thee whose blood can cleanse each spot,
   O Lamb of God, I come! I come!

3. Just as I am, Thou wilt receive,
   Wilt welcome, pardon, cleanse, relieve,
   Because Thy promise I believe,
   O Lamb of God, I come, I come!

Note: *It takes four Cherokee verses to translate three English verses.*

GUIDE ME, JEHOVAH

I. sgwa ti hni se sdi, yi ho wa,
e la di ga i suh i;
ji wa na ga hli yoo a yuh
ja hli ni gi di ni hi.
ni go...........hi luh..........
sgi sde li sge sdi yo go,
ni go...........hi luh ....
sgi sde li sge sdi yo go,

2. nuh wo ti ga luh go guh i
a nuh wo sgi sdoo i si:
a ji luh no oo lo gi luh
i guh yi a i se sdi.
sgi sde .... li sgi ....
di sgi ga na wa di da,
sgi sde .... li sgi ....
di sgi ga na wa di da.

3. ga la si nuh oo wa tla uh
jo da ni oo we yuh i,
sgi yo hi sda ne luh gwo no
a gwe li hi sdi sguh i;
sgi sde .... li sgi ....
do hi de sgi sa sta nuh,
ni go ....hi luh ....
do duh gi no gi sta ni.

TAKE THE NAME OF JESUS WITH YOU

Tune only

I. Take the name of Jesus with you,
Child of sorrow and of woe;
It will joy and comfort give you,
Take it then where'er you go.
Precious name, O how sweet!
Hope of earth and joy of heaven;
Precious name, O how sweet!
Hope of earth and joy of heaven.

2. Take the name of Jesus ever
As a shield from every snare;
If temptations ' round you gather,
Breathe that holy name in prayer.
Precious name, O how sweet!
Hope of earth and joy of heaven;
Precious name, O how sweet!
Hope of earth and joy of heaven.

3. At the name of Jesus bowing,
Falling prostrate at His feet,
King of kings in heaven we'll crown Him,
When our journey is complete.
Precious name , O how sweet!
Hope of earth and joy of heaven;
Precious name, O how sweet!
Hope of earth and joy of heaven.

See page 24 for same hymn in **Cherokee syllabary**

Translation:

Guide me, Jehovah, as I am walking through this barren land. I am weak, but Thou art Mighty. Forever hold us by Thy powerful hand.

Open now the crystal fountain whence the healing waters flow; and let the fiery cloud go before us, and lead us on our journey through.

When I tread the verge of the Jordan River, help me to still my fears. Bear me safely over and I shall sing Thy praises for eternity.

JESUS PAID IT ALL

I. uh tla go hoo sdi ya ha
i ya gwa duh ne di,
ji sa oo goo yuh ho nuh
a ya uh gi too guh.

chorus
ji sa a goo yuh,
ji sa ni ga duh
a yuh uh gi too guh i
a gwa goo yuh e luh.

2. ga luh lo joo dlo o se
joo luh wi sda ne di.
ni ga di oo swga do ne
i ya duh ne di yi.

3. ji sa noo duh ne luh i
ha li sga sdo ta nuh
guh di sgi, hna duh ne huh
ja hi hi ge se sdi.

4. ni ga duh ja de ho na
ji sa doo la sguh i,
na sgi hi ya li sga
o sduh ha le huh ga.

JESUS PAID IT ALL

Tune and translation

1. I hear the Saviour say,
"Thy strength indeed is small,
Child of weakness, watch and pray,
Find in Me thine all in all."

chorus
Jesus paid it all,
All to Him I owe;
Sin had left a crimson stain,
He washed it white as snow.

2. Lord, now indeed I find
Thy power, and Thine alone,
Can change the leper's spots,
And melt the heart of stone.

3. For nothing good have I
Whereby Thy grace to claim --
I'll wash my garments white
In the blood of Calvary's Lamb.

4. And when, before the throne,
I stand in Him complete,
"Jesus died my soul to save."
My lips shall still repeat.

ᏙᏓᎸ ᏅᏩᏙᎯᏯᏛ ᎬᏩᏂᎾᏕᎪᏫᏎᏱᏍᏗ ᏴᏫ,
ᎠᎴ ᏚᏜᎯᏝ ᏅᏩᏙᎯᏯᏛ ᎬᏩᏂᎾᏕᎪᏫᏎᏱᏍᏗ
ᏚᏳᎪᏛᎢ ᎢᏯᏛᏁᏗ ᎨᏒ ᎬᏗ.

ᏗᎧᏃᎩᏛ 72:3

THE MOUNTAINS SHALL BRING PEACE TO THE PEOPLE AND THE LITTLE HILLS BY RIGHTEOUSNESS.

PSALM 72 : 3

(Translated by Rev. Sanders McLemore, Stillwell, Oklahoma)

PRAISE TO THE SAVIOUR

1. sgi sde li sgi, juh suh hi yoo
   i juh luh gwo di sgo i,
   sgi sde li sge sdi gwo go ga
   ni go hi luh o je huh i.

chorus
   jo suh i wo ji ga ti, wo ji
   ga ti, oo ne hla nuh hi
   joo wo hluh i wo je he sdi
   hna gwa se ni go hi luh.

2. oo ne hla nuh hi oo we ji
   o ji luh gwo di sge sdi
   wo ji loo juh joo wo hluh i
   ga luh la di jo suh i.

3. oo wo doo hi i ga ge suh
   na hna da yo ji go hi,
   i yoo no a li sgwa duh ha
   e lo hi o je huh i.

4. oo ne hla nuh hi oo we ji
   o si o ji go ta huh,
   e lo hi da wa duh ho nuh
   oo li sgwa di di se sdi.

5. oo ni sga nuh juh hi oo yo
   duh a ni sga li ji sa,
   hna gwo ji sa ja i se sdi
   oo sga se sdi ge se sdi.

6. a se i da juh ni yuh hi
   sgi ya duh yuh duh ji sa;
   i juh ya li sga sdo de sdi
   i ga oo sga se duh i.

TWILIGHT IS FALLING

Tune only

I. Twilight is stealing over the sea,
   Shadows are falling dark on the lea;
   Borne on the night-winds, voices of yore,
   Come from the far-off shore.

chorus
   Far away beyond the star-lit skies,
   Where the lovelight never, never dies;
   Gleameth a mansion filled with delight,
   Sweet happy home so bright.

2. Voices of loved ones! songs of the past
   Still linger round me while life shall last,
   Lonely I wander, sadly I roam,
   Seeking that far-off home.

3. Come in the twilight, come, come to me,
   Bringing some message over the sea;
   Cheering my pathway, while here I roam,
   Seekinng that far-off home.

Translation

Thou alone art able to help us. We pray that Thou wilt continue to help us as long as we are in this present world.

We love (by the grace of the Almighty God) the Son of God and we shall ever praise Him to the highest.

We know that when the Lord and Saviour has finished calling out His people, we shall see a day more wonderful than that we have ever seen on this earth.

The Lord said, My way is the way of righteousnes. Whatsoever I have willed concerning the earth and all the inhabitants thereof, it shall be done.

Those who have gone contrary to the way of the Lord shall tremble before the Lord on the day when He shall come to pour out His judgement upon the wicked.

But those that belong to Him, He will in no wise cast out, and they shall not be afraid when He shall walk the earth in that day of His wrath.

CHRIST'S SECOND COMING

1. oo ne hla nuh hi oo we ji
   i ga goo yuh he i,
   hna gwo jo suh wi oo lo se
   i ga goo yuh ho nuh.

2. a se no i oo ne je i
   i yoo no doo le nuh,
   ta li ne duh ji loo ji li
   oo duh hne oo ne juh.

3. e la ni guh duh li sgwa di
   ga loo juh ha i yoo
   ni ga duh da ye di go i
   a hni e la ni guh.

4. oo na da nuh ti a ne huh
   do duh ya nuh hi li,
   jo suh na gwo ni go hi luh
   to hi wa ne he sdi.

AMAZING GRACE

(tune only)

1. Amazing grace! how sweet the sound,
   That saved a wretch like me!
   I once was lost, but now am found.
   Was blind, but now I see.

2. ' Twas grace that taught my heart to fear,
   And grace my fears relieved;
   How precious did that grace appear
   The hour I first believed!

3. Thro' many dangers, toils and snares,
   I have already come;
   'Tis grace hath brought me safe thus far,
   And grace will lead me home.

4. When we've been there ten thousand years,
   Bright shining as the sun,
   We've no less days to sing God's praise
   Than when we first begun.

See page 13 for this same song in **Cherokee Syllabary**

Translation:

The Son of God paid the price for our redemption. When He finished (His death, burial and ressurection), making the payment, and He ascended into heaven(after forty days).

But before He ascended into heaven, He said, "Let not your heart be troubled; ye believe in God, believe also in me. In my Father's house are many mansions: if it were not so, I would have told you. I go to prepare a place for you. And if I go to prepare a place for you, I will come again, and receive you unto myself, that where I am, there ye may be also."

And when he comes again, (Beloved, now we are the sons of God, and it doth not yet appear what we shall be, but we know that, when he shall appear, we shall be like Him) we shall see Him as He is.

And all they who live in righteousness of the Lord Jesus Christ, and shall continue in love, will live in peace in heaven for eternity.

GUIDE ME, JEHOVAH

May be sung to the tune **Precious Memories**

<table>
<tr>
<td>
l. sgwa ti hni se sdi, yi ho wa,
e la di ga i suh i;
ji wa na ga li yoo a yuh,
ja hli ni gi di ni hi,
ni go hi luh, ni go hi luh,
sgi sde li sge sdi yo go;
ni go hi luh, ni go hi luh,
sgi sde li sge sdi yo go.
</td>
<td>
ᏍᏆᏘᏂᏎᏍᏗ, ᏱᎰᏩ,
ᎡᎳᏗ ᎦᎢᏒᎢ;
ᏥᏩᎾᎦᎵᏳ ᎠᏴ,
ᏣᎵᏂᎩᏗ ᏂᎯ.
ᏂᎪᎯᎸ, ᏂᎪᎯ ,
ᏍᎩᏍᏕᎵᏍᎨᏍᏗᏲᎪ;
ᏂᎪᎯᎸ, ᏂᎪᎯᎸ,
ᏍᎩᏍᏕᎵᏍᎨᏍᏗᏲᎪ.
</td>
</tr>
<tr>
<td>
2. nuh wo ti ga luh go guh i
a nuh wo sgi sdoo i si;
a ji luh no oo lo gi luh
i guh yi a i se sdi.
sgi sde li sgi, sgi sde li sgi,
di sgi ga na wa di da;
sgi sde li sgi, sgi sde li sgi,
di sgi ga na wa di da.
</td>
<td>
ᏅᏬᏘ ᎦᎸᎪᎬᎢ
ᎠᏅᏬ ᏍᎩᏍᏚᎢᏏ;
ᎠᏥᎸᏃ ᎤᎶᎩᎸ
ᎢᎬᏱ ᎠᎢᏎᏍᏗ.
ᏍᎩᏍᏕ ᏍᎩ, ᏍᎩᏍᏕᎵᏍᎩ,
ᏗᏍᎩᎦᎾᏩᏗᏓ;
ᏍᎩᏍᏕᎵᏍᎩ, ᏍᎩᏍᏕᎵᏍᎩ,
ᏗᏍᎩᎦᎾᏩᏗᏓ.
</td>
</tr>
<tr>
<td>
3. ga la si nuh oo wa tla uh
jo da ni oo we yuh i,
sgi yo hi sda ne luh gwo no
a gwe li hi sdi sguh i;
sgi sde li sgi, sgi sde li sgi,
to hi de sgi sa sta nuh;
ni go hi luh, ni go hi luh,
to da guh no gi sta ni.
</td>
<td>
ᎦᎳᏏᏅ ᎤᏩᏝᎥ
ᏦᏓᏂ ᎤᏪᏴᎢ,
ᏍᎩᏲᎯᏍᏓᏁᎸᏉᏃ
ᎠᏇᎵᎯᏍᏗᏍᎬᎢ;
ᏍᎩᏍᏕᎵᏍᎩ, ᏍᎩᏍᏕᎵᏍᎩ,
ᏙᎯ ᏕᏍᎩᏌᏍᏔᏅ;
ᏂᎪᎯᎸ, ᏂᎪᎯᎸ,
ᏙᏓᎬᏃᎩᏍᏔᏂ.
</td>
</tr>
</table>

See also page 13

Translation:

Guide me, Jehovah, as I am walking through this barren land. I am weak, but Thou art mighty. Forever hold us in Thy powerful hand.

Open now the crystal fountain whence the healing waters flow; and let the fiery cloud go before us, and lead us on our journey through.

When I tread the verge of the Jordan River, help me to still my fears. Bear me safely over and I shall sing Thy praises for eternity.

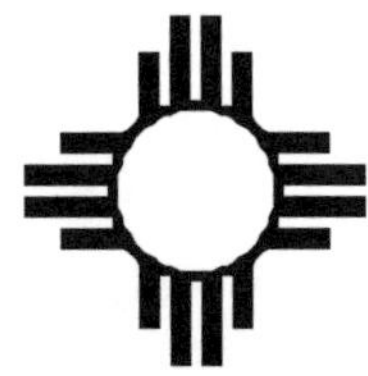

Amazing Grace

Cherokee
OOH NAY THLA NAH, HEE OO WAY GEE.'
E GAH GWOO YAH HAY EE.
NAW GWOO JOE SAH, WE YOU LOW SAY,
E GAH GWOO YAH HO NAH.

Navajo
NIZHÓNÍGO JOOBA' DITTS' A'
YISDÁSHÍÍTÍNÍGÍÍ,
LAH YÓÓÍÍYÁ, K'AD SHÉNÁHOOSDZIN,
DOO EESH'ĮĮ DA ŃT'ÉÉ.

Kiowa
DAW K'EE DA HA DAWTSAHY HE TSOW'HAW
DAW K'EE DA HA DAWTSAHY HEE.
BAY DAWTSAHY TAW, GAW AYM OW THAH T'AW,
DAW K'EE DA HA DAWTSAHY H'EE.

Creek
PO YA FEK CHA HE THLAT AH TET
AH NON AH CHA PA KAS
CHA FEE KEE O FUNNAN LA KUS
UM E HA TA LA YUS.

Choctaw
SHILOMBISH HOLITOPA MA!
ISHMMINTI PULLA CHA
HATAK ILBUSHA PIA HA
IS PI YUKPALASHKE.

WORDS: John Newton, 1779; st. 6 anon.; phonetic transcription Cherokee, Kiowa, Creek, Choctaw as sung in Oklahoma Indian Missionary Conference; Navajo phonetic transcription by Albert Tsosie (1 Chr. 17:16-17)
MUSIC: 19th cent. USA melody; harm. by Edwin O. Excell, 1900

AMAZING GRACE
CM

LOVE TO JESUS

1. oo ja ti ji ge yoo a
ji sa ga loo ne duh;
na sgi a gi sde li sgi
a gwa goo yuh duh no.
na sgi ji luh gwo di
ni go hi li ge uh (i),
a le ji no he sge sdi
oo da do li ja duh.

2. a gi sde li sgi ji sa
ga luh la di jo suh
nuh joo da le nuh huh na
ga luh gwo di e he (hi);
na hna a ne huh i
na sgi doo la sguh i
i guh yi tluh e la di
guh wa da nuh ne he (i).

3. a se no oo ja ta nuh
oo sgwa ni go di yoo
oo da do li ja duh i
ji ji go wa ti ha !
ga luh gwo di ge suh (i)
hna gwo oo wa de juh;
yi ho wa no oo we ji
yuh wi ni ga li sda.

4. yuh wi a ne do huh i
e la di e do ha,
o si ni ga duh ne ha
yuh wi ni go hi luh.
guh wa ni sgwa ti huh (i)
tla ya ga sa ya sdi (ha),
o si ni ga duh ne ha
na soo li go guh na

NEAR THE CROSS

Tune only

1. Jesus, keep me near the cross,
There a precious fountain
Free to all -- a healing stream,
Flows from Calv'ry's mountain.
In the cross, in the cross,
Be my glory ever;
Till my raptured soul shall find
Rest beyond the river.

2. Near the cross, a trembling soul,
Love and mercy found me;
There the Bright and Morning Star
Sheds its beams around me.
In the cross, in the cross,
Be my glory ever;
Till my raptured soul shall find
Rest beyond the river.

3. Near the cross ! O Lamb of God,
Bring its scenes before me;
Help me walk from day to day,
With its shadows o'er me.
In the cross, in the cross,
Be my glory ever;
Till my raptured soul shall find
Rest beyond the river.

4. Near the cross I'll watch and wait,
Hoping, trusting ever,
Till I reach the golden strand,
Just beyond the river.
In the cross, in the cross,
Be my glory ever;
Till my raptured soul shall find
Rest beyond the river.

May also be sung to: **Jesus Saves**

Translation:

I love the Lord Jesus Christ with great joy. He is my help; He paid my debt to God; that is why I shall always love Him. I shall tell of His love, mercy and grace.

He is my help and has loved me from eternity past. The angels are His and He made all the things in heaven and in earth.

Because of His great mercy, He has sealed His children to Himself. He was made flesh that we might behold Him.

He walked on the earth as man and fulfilled the law. He lay down His life on the cross at Calvary to pay in full the sin debt of His people; that by His shed blood we are declared righteous. For without shedding of blood, there is no remission.

GOD ALL IN ALL

1. guh ge yoo i sgwa ne hla nuh
ni hi juh suh hi yoo
ga luh la di a le e lo (hi)
guh ya doo li sgo i;
ga luh la di a le e lo (hi)
guh ya doo li sgo i.

2. a se gwo gwo ji noo da le
goo hoo sdi ni ga uh:
uh tla nuh wa do hi ya duh
guh gi ne di yi gi.
uh tla nuh wa do hi ya duh,
guh gi ne di yi gi.

3. joo guh wa lo di ja gi ha
sgi ne ha juh suh hi (yoo),
juh suh a le de sgi ka ne (ha)
na sgwo di gwa li i.
juh suh a le de sgi ka ne (ha)
na sgwo di gwa li i.

4. a se no tla di gwa li i
a le go hoo sdi gwo
di guh tli lo sdo di yi gi
a gwa hne hla nuh hi.
di guh tli lo sdo di yi gi,
a gwa hne hla nuh hi.

ALL HAIL THE POWER

Tune only

1. All hail the power of Jesus' name!
Let angels prostrate fall;
Bring forth the royal diadem,
And crown Him Lord of all;
Bring forth the royal diadem,
And crown Him Lord of all!

2. Ye chosen seed of Israel's race,
Ye ransomed from the fall,
Hail Him who saves you by His grace,
And crown Him Lord of all.
Hail Him who saves you by His grace,
And crown Him Lord of all.

3. Let every kindred, every tribe,
On this terrestrial ball,
To Him all majesty ascribe,
And crown Him Lord of all;
To Him all majesty ascribe,
And crown Him Lord of all

4. O that with yonder sacred throng
We at His feet may fall!
We'll join the everlasting song,
And crown Him Lord of all;
We'll join the everlasting song,
And crown Him Lord of all.

Translation:

Psalm 63

O God Thou art my God; early will I seek Thee. My soul thirsteth for Thee, my flesh longeth for Thee in a dry and thirsty land, where no water is, to seeThy power and Thy glory, so as I have seen Thee in the sanctuary.

Because Thy loving kindness is better than life, my lips shall praise Thee. Thus will I bless Thee while I live. I will lift up my hands in Thy name.

My soul shall be satisfied as with marrow and fatness; and my mouth shall praise Thee with joyful lips, when I remember Thee upon my bed, and meditate on Thee in the night watches.

Because Thou hast been my help, therefore, in the shadow of Thy wings will I rejoice. My soul followeth hard after Thee; Thy right hand upholdeth me. But those that seek my soul, to destroy it, shall go into the lower parts of the earth.

They shall fall by the sword; they shall be a portion for foxes. But the king shall rejoice in God; every one that sweareth by him shall glory: but the mouth of them that speak lies shall be stopped.

CHEROKEE

Ed Sharpe Sr., Kay Sharpe

music copy & notation by Ed Sharpe Jr.

THERE IS A FOUNTAIN

1. ga noo go guh a ni sga na
oo na da wo sdi yi,
na hna oo na do soo le di
oo ni sga nuh juh i,
oo ni sga nuh juh i.
oo ni sga nuh juh i;
na hna oo na do soo le di,
oo ni sga nuh juh i.

2. ji sa ye no ga lo ne duh
gi g(a) oo je wo je le i,
na sgi oo gi guh na ni uh
oo ni nuh ga li sgi.
oo ni nuh ga li sgi,
oo ni nuh ga li sgi;
na sgi oo gi guh na ni uh,
oo ni nuh ga li sgi.

3. ja yo hoo sge oo sga nuh juh
a da na sa huh sgi
oo li he li je oo go huh
na sgi ga noo go guh.
na sgi ga noo go guh,
na sgi ga noo go guh;
oo li he li je oo go huh,
na sgi ga noo go guh.

4. na sgwo a yuh ji sga na i
na hna ga noo go guh
ji loo gi ga li e li guh
ga do soo le i ga.
ga do soo le i ga,
ga do soo le i ga;
ji loo gi ga li e li ga,
ga do soo le i ga.

5. oo gi guh joo je wo je le(i)
ji sa ga lo ne duh
ji yo oo suh ha guh di sgi
de ji no gi sdi ha.
de ji no gi sdi ha,
de ji no gi sdi ha;
ji yo oo suh ha guh di sgi,
de ji no gi sdi ha.

THERE IS A FOUNTAIN

Tune and translation

1. There is a fountain filled with blood
Drawn from Immanuel's veins;
And sinners, plunged beneath that flood,
Lose all their guilty stains:
Lose all their guilty stains,
Lose all their guilty stains;
And sinners plunged beneath that flood,
Lose all their guilty stains.

2. The dying thief rejoiced to see
That fountain in his day;
And there may I, though vile as he,
Wash all my sins away:
Wash all my sins away,
Wash all my sins away;
And there may I, though vile as he,
Wash all my sins away.

3. Dear dying Lamb, Thy precious blood
Shall never lose its power,
Till all the ransomed Church of God
Be saved, to sin no more:
Be saved, to sin no more,
Be saved, to sin no more;
Till all the ransomed Church of God,
Be saved to sin no more.

4. E'er since by faith I saw the stream
Thy flowing wound supply,
Redeeming love has been my theme,
And shall be'till I die:.
And shall be'till I die,
And shall be'till I die;
Redeeming love has been my theme,
And shall be 'till I die.

5. When this poor lisping, stam'ring tongue
Lies silent in the grave,
Then in a nobler, sweeter song,
I'll sing Thy power to save;
I'll sing Thy power to save,
I'll sing Thy power to save;
Then in a nobler, sweeter song,
I'll sing Thy power to save.

WHAT GOD HAS DONE FOR ME

1. a ni yo i ji loo gi e ja goo yuh duh
ni ga duh i ja duh da sde sdi yi,
da juh no he he li noo li he li sduh i
a yuh ji sa a gi do li juh i.

ga luh la di e hi ji sga nuh je luh -
gi, joo yo dluh wi ga na noo go guh
a ya noo li a gwa de do wa di suh gi,
go hoo sdi ni ji na ye sguh na i.

2. oo ne hla nuh hi oo da do li ja duh i
a si e la di ji ga le ne ha;
oo ja ta nuh hi sgi ni oo sgwa ni go di
juh sgi no wi ni ge uh na ji gi.

oo ja ta nuh oo li si guh ji nuh guh
ni ge li sguh na wi ji ga duh i;
a sgi no oo doo li sguh a gwa ti hni suh,
a le tla yi ji ni gwa ti he i.

3. ki la ga luh gwo di yi ho wa oo ne juh
a yuh a gwa le wi sdo ta nuh huh,
"ja sga nuh juh ha ga ta huh na," oo duh hnuh,
"ga do gwo no duh hi yo hoo si gwo ?"

a gwa da nuh do hna gwo oo duh hni duh -
hi, a gi yo hoo suh doo le hnuh gi;
i je di ka no gi duh da gwuh ta nuh gi;
ji sa de ji no gi sta nuh gi yi.

PRAISE HIM ! PRAISE HIM !

Fanny J. Crosby

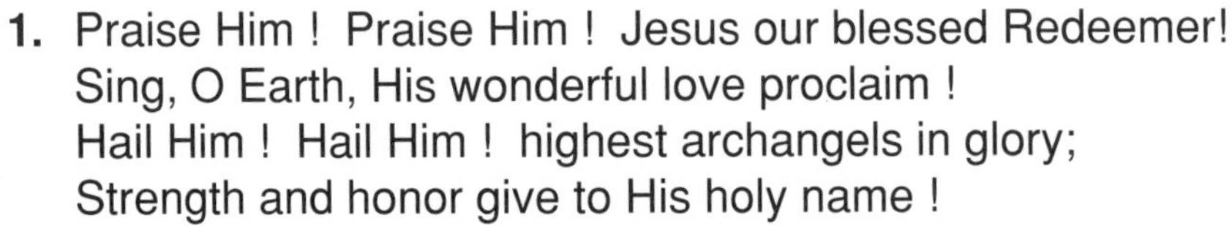

1. Praise Him ! Praise Him ! Jesus our blessed Redeemer!
Sing, O Earth, His wonderful love proclaim !
Hail Him ! Hail Him ! highest archangels in glory;
Strength and honor give to His holy name !

Like a shepherd, Jesus will guard His children,
In His arms He carries them all day long:
Praise Him ! Praise Him ! Tell of His excellent greatness:
Praise Him ! Praise Him ! ever in joyful song !

2. Praise Him ! Praise Him ! Jesus our blessed Redeemer!
For our sins He suffered , and bled, and died;
He our Rock, our hope of eternal salvation,
Hail Him ! Hail Him ! Jesus the Crucified.

Sound His praises ! Jesus who bore our sorrows,
Love unbounded, wonderful, deep and strong:
Praise Him ! Praise Him ! Tell of His excellent greatness:
Praise Him ! Praise Him ! ever in joyful song !

HEAVEN BEAUTIFUL

1. oo ne hla nuh hi oo we ji ni ga di
e di ge yoo hi, hna gwo di da le huh,
woo lo suh i da i se sdi, de ga da -
ni yuh se sdi no, di ga da ge yoo hi.

chorus * *denotes base and alto only*

ga luh lo yoo wo doo
*ga luh lo, ga luh lo: yoo wo doo
yoo wo doo

na ni we yi ho wa
*na ni we, na ni we: yi ho wa, yi ho wa

joo je li a sga ni
*joo je li, joo je li: a sga ni, a sga ni

ne huh na
*ne huh na, ne huh na,
jo suh i, na hna ni.

2. oo guh wi yoo hi oo je li de di ka -
hna wa di se sdi a hni e loh ge suh;
sa gwo no noo sdi di se sdi; ji sa ga -
lo ne duh na sgi de ga ti ni se sdi.

3. o sduh i gi do li juh hi e da li -
e li je he sdi ni go hi luh hna gwo;
yoo do hi yoo yi gi ye luh a se i -
gi sde luh di gwo, oo ne juh hi ye no.

4. oo ne hla nuh hi oo we ji joo we do-
li sdi gwo a se guh wa ta yo se hi;
i ga tuh ga nuh hi ye no noo sduh gwo
i de huh a hni, oo yo sduh gwo ye no.

5. ye di la si ti ha ji sa, oo yo i -
ga li sda ne di hna gwa se, oo ne juh,
noo no hi yoo nuh na yi gi da yoo
na le na li a se, oo duh hnuh hi ji sa.

6. oo ne hla nuh hi oo we ji hi a ni -
gi we se le i; a yuh sgi sta wa doo,
da ji hwa tuh hi gwo a se wi nas duh -
na i ga ga ti ga luh la di jo suh.

1. Let us, who love the Son of God, rise up and follow Him in love.

2. Let us look to the ways of the Lord while we are still on this earth, and the Lord Jesus Christ shall lead us.

3. Let us continually give thanks unto Him who had mercy upon us.

4. The Son of God came into the world. The world was evil; the world knew Him not. He called and we heard Him.

5. Some doubted that He was the Christ because their way was evil. Jesus said that there will be those who would never know the way.

6. The Son of God said, "Follow thou me." We have heard His voice and we shall follow Him.

SEQUOYAH
Creator of the Cherokee Syllabary

TWENTY THIRD PSALM
In Cherokee Syllabary

ᏗᎧᏃᎩᏛ 23

ᏱᎰᏩ ᎠᏆᏤᎵ ᎠᏫ ᏗᎦᏘᏯ; ᎥᏝ ᏱᎬᎩᏂᎪᎯᏎᏉᏍᏗ.

ᎢᏤ ᎦᎦᎸᎸᏒ ᎠᎩᏂᏌᏬᏍᎪ ᎾᏍᎩ; ᎠᏆᏘᏂᏕ ᎤᏮᏗᏢ
ᎤᏓᏥᎾᏍᏛ ᎠᎹ ᎦᎦᏍᏁᏬᎢ.

ᎠᏆᏓᏅᏙ ᏔᎵᏁ ᎠᏗᏃᎯᎬᎢ; ᎠᏆᏘᏂᏕ ᏚᏩᎪᏛ
ᎦᎦᎤᎤᎢ, ᎤᏗᎦᏓᏍᏙᏗᏍᎪ ᎤᏩᏒ ᏚᏙᎥᎢ.

ᎾᏍᏉ ᏱᎦᎢ ᎤᎨᏓᎵᏴ ᎤᏓᏩᏗᏍᏙᏛ ᎠᏂᎢᎯᏍᏗ
ᎨᏒᎢ ᎠᏎ ᎥᏝ ᏴᎦᏥᏍᎦᏯ ᎪᎢᏍᏗ ᎤᏲᎢ, ᏂᎯᏰᏃ
ᎦᏍᎩᎾᏓᏩᏗᏙᎬᎢ; ᏂᎯ ᏣᏤᎵ ᎦᎾᏍᏓ ᎠᎴ ᏂᎯ
ᏣᏤᎵ ᎠᏙᏔᏅᏍᏗ ᎬᎩᎦᎵᏍᏓᏗᏍᎪᎢ.

ᏂᎯ ᎢᎬᏱᏢ ᏍᏆᏛᎾᎢᏍᏓᏁᎲ ᎦᏍᎩᎸᎢ ᎠᏂᎦᏔᎲ
ᎬᎩᏍᎦᎩ; ᏂᎯ ᎪᎢ ᎯᎶᏁᏗᏍᎪ ᏥᏍᎪᎵ; ᎠᏆᏤᎵ
ᎤᎵᏍᏈᏗ ᎠᏧᏢᎪᎢ.

ᏄᎴᏌᏛᏒᎾ ᎣᏍᏛ ᎠᎴ ᎤᏓᏙᎵᏍᏗ ᎨᏒ ᎬᎩᏍᏓᏩᏗᏙ-
ᎮᏍᏗ ᏂᎪᎯᎸ ᎨᎥᎢ, ᎠᎴ ᎠᏎ ᏂᎪᎯᎸ ᏥᏍᏒᏍᏗ
ᏱᎰᏩ ᎤᏤᎵ ᎠᏓᏁᎸᎢ.